# STORMZY
## THE ULTIMATE FAN BOOK

Published in the UK by Scholastic Children's Books, 2020
Euston House, 24 Eversholt Street, London, NW1 1DB
A division of Scholastic Limited

London ~ New York ~ Toronto ~ Sydney ~ Auckland
Mexico City ~ New Delhi ~ Hong Kong

Written by Emily Hibbs © Scholastic Children's Books, 2020

ISBN 978 0702 30519 1

Printed and bound by Bell & Bain Ltd, UK

2 4 6 8 10 9 7 5 3 1

www.scholastic.co.uk

# STORMZY

## THE ULTIMATE FAN BOOK

SCHOLASTIC

# CONTENTS

# INTRODUCTION

Everybody has heard of Stormzy. In just a few years, he has transformed from a talented hopeful to one of the biggest artists in the UK. With two number-one albums, four BRIT Awards and an iconic Glastonbury performance, Stormzy is determined to keep pushing himself, and pushing boundaries, until he achieves everything he has set out to do. But Stormzy's legacy goes beyond music. Unafraid to speak out about things that matter to him and call out injustice when he sees it, his passion, activism and faith are part of what makes him such a powerful voice for his generation.

In this book you can discover the story behind Stormzy's rise to fame, as well as finding out all about his friends, influences and the future of #Merky. There's also space to write your own bars and see how well you know the king of grime in the ultimate Stormzy quiz.

# ALL ABOUT STORMZY

Name: **Michael Ebenazer Kwadjo Omari Owuo Jr**

Performer name: **Stormzy**

Nicknames: **Big Michael, The Problem, Wicked Skengman**

Date of Birth: **26th July 1993**

Born in: **Croydon, South London**

Famous as: **rapper, singer and songwriter**

## FOLLOW STORMZY

Keep up to date with Stormzy on social media.

**Snapchat:** Stormzy1

**YouTube:** Stormzy

## STAY SAFE ONLINE

Social media apps like Snapchat and Instagram are great ways to keep in touch with friends and stay up to date with your favourite influencers. However, it's important to be smart and stay safe online. Don't give out personal details like your full name, address or school and never request these details from anyone else. Don't upload photos in your school uniform, as that might allow people to pinpoint your location. Many social media apps say that users must be at least 13 years old before creating an account or using the app in any way. If an app or website has an age restriction then don't ignore it (they have them for a reason!) and report any comments that make you feel uncomfortable to a trusted adult.

# THE STORMZY STORY SO FAR

## THE START OF THE STORY

Stormzy was born as Michael Omari Jr in Croydon, South London. He grew up in nearby Thornton Heath with his Ghanaian mum, Abigail, and two sisters, Sylvia and Rachael, and younger half-brother, Brandon. Times were sometimes hard – Stormzy's dad wasn't around and his mum had to work several jobs to look after them – but the family were close and stuck together when things got tough.

A regular churchgoer, Stormzy was also part of the Boys' Brigade, a Christian organization similar to the Scouts. He even played the bugle in the brigade's marching band, though he admits he didn't practise much so wasn't very good at it!

Stormzy was motivated even when he was little and dreamed of becoming the prime minister one day. He may not have ended up as a member of parliament, but this early ambition would see him reach great heights.

## EARLY INSPIRATION

Though his family wasn't especially musical, Stormzy was still surrounded by inspiration from a young age. He got to know gospel music through his church and listened to his sister's favourite genre of R&B blasting out of the CD player in her bedroom. Later, he was inspired by artists on Channel U, an urban radio station that launched the careers of stars including Tinchy Stryder, Tinie Tempah, Dizzee Rascal and Nasty Crew.

Channel U gave a platform to artists that didn't have massive followings, or weren't signed to big music labels, and showed Stormzy that people from similar backgrounds and similar areas to him had a chance of being in the spotlight.

## LEARNING TO SPIT

When he was eleven years old, Stormzy started freestyling and battle rapping at local youth clubs. Here, he would spit some off-the-cuff verses before another challenger grabbed the mic. From these clashes, Stormzy honed his rapping skills and started to develop his own style. Soon, he was not only winning the battles, but getting a reputation outside of the youth clubs.

## CHILD OF GRIME

Stormzy's style was influenced by grime artists like Wiley, Dizzee Rascal and Skepta, who he grew up listening to on Channel U. Grime music emerged from a fusion of British rap, Jamaican reggae, garage and jungle, but has a distinctive sound all its own. It developed in London in the 1990s and soon became a popular genre all over the UK.

Still, for many years, most radio stations and music labels dismissed grime as being too fast, or too hardcore, to appeal to mainstream audiences.

## SCHOOL DAYS

Stormzy attended Harris Academy in South Norwood, London, where he enjoyed school life. English Literature was one of his best subjects and he loved reading books in his free time. His favourite novel was *Noughts and Crosses* by Malorie Blackman – a love story about two teenagers growing up in a society where darker-skinned Crosses are superior to lighter-skinned Noughts.

Stormzy shone in most subjects but wasn't always a model student in terms of behaviour! He was often cheeky, chatting back to teachers and getting into trouble. Once, he even threw a sandwich at his friend's head during assembly! Despite this, he did well in his GCSEs, getting six A*s and achieving the highest grades in his year.

## STARTING OUT ON YOUTUBE

Wanting to reach a wider audience than just his circle of friends, Stormzy started putting out YouTube videos. His first ever vid, uploaded in 2011, was called "Mike Lowrey".
In it, Stormzy freestyled over a grime instrumental. His video may have only got a few hundred views to start with, but Stormzy kept at it.

## A ROCKY ROAD

In some areas of Thornton Heath, violent crime was rife. For many young people, it was hard to escape this violence and several of Stormzy's friends got mixed up in dangerous lifestyles. Stormzy ended up in trouble with the police on a couple of occasions and was also the victim of serious crime. He was stabbed three times. All around him, Stormzy saw friends and classmates who had little hope. Because they couldn't see a way of achieving their dreams, they gave up on them. But Stormzy always had faith and confidence that things could be different one day. He refused to give up on his own dreams.

## WAKE-UP CALL

After doing so brilliantly in his GCSEs, college was a bit of a shock for Stormzy. He didn't enjoy classes so much and his grades slipped. He realized that intelligence and talent would

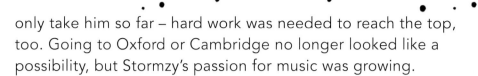

only take him so far – hard work was needed to reach the top, too. Going to Oxford or Cambridge no longer looked like a possibility, but Stormzy's passion for music was growing.

## WHAT NEXT?

Stormzy ended up getting expelled from college for his behaviour. He enrolled at another college for a couple of months, but then decided he'd rather get a job and start earning. He took on an engineering apprenticeship in Leamington Spa before starting a placement at an oil refinery in Southampton. Though he was making good money and learning a new skill, the role wasn't fulfilling. He missed South London and missed making music.

During a rare week off, he put together his first mixtape, named *168*, which featured a selection of tracks written and recorded in just seven days (168 hours).

A couple of months later, one of Stormzy's favourite grime duos, Krept & Konan, won Best UK Newcomer at the 2013 MOBO (Music of Black Origin) Awards. Konan was from Thornton Heath and Krept had gone to Stormzy's school. Most other grime stars were from North or East London, so to see a duo from South London reach such heights gave Stormzy hope. It made him realize that if Krept and Konan could make it big so could he.

## HEADING HOME

Stormzy had a tough choice to make. Did he stay on his secure but unsatisfactory career path, or did he take a leap of faith and try to make it in the music industry? Inspired by Krept & Konan's success, Stormzy decided to quit his job and come home. He was ready to focus on his music.

He started releasing his Wicked Skengman freestyle videos on YouTube, with the first landing in November 2013. Slowly but surely, his videos got more hits and Stormzy built up a loyal following.

## GETTING NOTICED

With the help of some of his good friends, Stormzy continued putting out freestyle videos. All across London, and further afield, secondary-school kids were watching his videos, sharing his posts and rapping along to his bars.

His uploads were now getting thousands of hits, and he also had a huge following on Twitter and Snapchat. As his reputation grew, big brands started to take notice. He became an ambassador for Adidas,

sporting their gear in his videos.

## STAYING INDEPENDENT

Music labels soon spotted the rising star doing the rounds on social media and invited Stormzy in for meetings. But rather than sign with an established manager, Stormzy asked his friend Tobe to take on the role instead. Tobe didn't have much experience, but he was smart and good at networking. Most crucially, he shared Stormzy's dreams. Stormzy believed it was more important to work with someone he knew and trusted than someone with a big name. Tobe got to work straight away, reaching out to any contacts that might be able to help, and soon had Stormzy booked for several shows at universities.

*"Every single thing that I was told that I couldn't do without a label – get in the charts, get on to the Radio 1 playlist – I've done."*

—Stormzy

# MAKING MUSIC

By 2014, things began to pick up. Stormzy released his first EP, *Dreamer's Disease*, won his first MOBO award for Best Grime Act and became the first unsigned grime artist to appear on *Later… with Jools Holland*. In November, he had his first major collaboration, appearing on the track "I'm Fine" alongside Chip.

The #Merky team was born. For a while it was just the two of them – Stormzy made the music, and Tobe spoke to venues, sorted logistics and contacted the press. But as Stormzy's success soared, Tobe struggled to manage everything on his own. It wouldn't be long before they needed to grow the team.

# SHUT UP

A defining moment for Stormzy came when Kanye West invited him on stage during his performance at the 2015 BRIT Awards, along with around forty other stars from the grime world. For some people, this was a powerful salute to the underground music scene, but others scoffed at the move on social media, calling Stormzy and the rest of the grime artists "back-up dancers". In response, Stormzy wrote the track "Shut Up". Performed in a local park and videoed on a handheld camera, Stormzy told his haters where to go. The video got over 100,000 views within just a few weeks.

In March 2015, Stormzy released his single "Know Me From" with a music video featuring his mum!
The track went viral on YouTube and reached the top 50 in the UK charts.

## RISING STAR

In December, Stormzy performed "Shut Up" at the O2 Arena, ahead of boxer Anthony Joshua's fight against Dillian Whyte for the British heavyweight title. The track rocketed up the charts. Stormzy started a social media campaign to take it to a Christmas number one. Though the track may not have got the top spot, it made number eight – a massive achievement for an independent grime artist!

The Stormzy brand was now too big for Tobe to manage on his own. The #Merky family grew by several members, including a publicist, a lawyer, a booking agent and a tour manager. Many of those hired had been Stormzy's friends from childhood, or friends of friends, as it was important that the people he worked with shared his views and vision.

With his trusted team assembled, Stormzy was ready to reach greater heights. Now his ideas, once dreams, became real possibilities. Social media was still a key part of getting Stormzy's music and his name out there but now he was also being booked for interviews and photoshoots with big publications. However, Stormzy was worried that his reputation was bigger than his achievements. He knew he had the talent to match some of the most popular stars out there but didn't feel like his work had shown it yet. Now, he was ready to do something EPIC.

## STRIVING FOR EXCELLENCE

For ten months in 2016, Stormzy largely went off the radar to work on his first album. He already had lots of good ideas for track titles and lyrics, but he wanted the album to be more than good. He wanted it to be excellent.

Putting the album together was tough, both mentally and physically, and there were weeks at a time when he'd isolate himself and wouldn't even answer calls from friends, family or even his then-girlfriend, TV presenter Maya Jama.

It was so important to Stormzy that he got this right. Rather than playing it safe, he wanted to experiment with different genres, bring in collaborators and show a range of styles. Perhaps most importantly, he wanted to speak directly to his younger fans and inspire them to achieve their own dreams.

## FEELING LOW

While working on his first album, Stormzy suffered from depression, a condition that causes people to feel very low and hopeless. He rapped about his struggle on a few tracks, including "Lay Me Bare", and chatted about his mental health in later interviews. Though he found it difficult to talk about, Stormzy felt it was important to share his story and let others going through similar situations know that they weren't alone.

*"It's been a very messy journey so far ... I want that journey embodied in my album. I want to show every bit of my character. You'll hear my darkest thoughts and deepest secrets. I'll be saying, 'This is me, Mike.'"*

—Stormzy, GQ Magazine (2017)

# #GSAP

At the start of 2017, billboards began popping up all over London bearing powerful quotes and displaying the sign off *#GSAP*. On 24th February, *Gang Signs & Prayer* dropped. Raw, honest and heartfelt, Stormzy used the sixteen tracks to tell his story so far.

With elements of gospel, R&B and, of course, grime, the album was an instant success with fans and critics. It sold over 68,000 copies in its first week, broke the record for the most first-week streams for a British artist and quickly hit the number-one spot in the album charts. From the powerful gospel track "Blinded by Your Grace Part 2", to the chill R&B tune "Cigarettes & Cush", to the hardcore tribute to grime "Bad Boys", there was something on there for everyone. Stormzy had strived for, and achieved, excellence. He was proud to have created an album that lived up to his massive reputation.

Just before his first album was released, Stormzy moved into a new flat in upmarket Chelsea, West London. He'd only been there a couple of weeks, however, when neighbours called the police on him, thinking he was a burglar. The police broke down his door to gain entry. The misunderstanding was quickly sorted out, but many questioned whether the incident had racist undertones, and whether it would have happened if Stormzy wasn't Black.

Also in 2017, Stormzy travelled the country with his sell-out *#GSAP* tour, launched the #Merky Festival in Ibiza, gained two more MOBOs and won the Artist of the Year at the BBC Music Awards.

## BRINGING IT AT THE BRITS

Stormzy was a star. Now, it wasn't just a few secondary-school kids watching his videos on the back of the bus – he had become a household name, with millions of fans young and old. For many, Stormzy was more than music. He showed just what could be achieved with passion, dedication and ambition. He had risen up to become something huge.

Nobody could accuse Stormzy of being a back-up dancer at the 2018 BRIT Awards. He took centre stage with a performance that would go down in his history. Not only did he give incredible renditions of "Blinded by Your Grace Part 2" and "Big for Your Boots", but he also dropped a memorable freestyle in support of the victims of the Grenfell fire. Stormzy ended the night with two BRIT Awards for British Male Solo Artist and British Album of the Year for *Gang Signs & Prayer*.

In June 2017, a terrible fire broke out in Grenfell Tower, a block of flats in West London. Seventy-two people died as a result of the tragedy.

# #MERKY BOOKS

Stormzy's vision had always been that #Merky would go beyond music and, in 2018, he launched #Merky Books, part of publishing company Penguin Random House for writers from diverse backgrounds. One of the first titles they published was *Rise Up* – a book charting Stormzy's career so far. Rather than a straightforward account of his rise to fame, Stormzy asked several members of his team to share their own life stories and experiences, too.

# NUMBER-ONE SINGLE

In April 2019, Stormzy released the single "Vossi Bop", along with a music video set in different locations around London, including Westminster Bridge. It was an instant hit, beating Taylor Swift's newest single for the top spot in the UK charts, and was streamed over twelve million times in its debut week!

The title of the song comes from the name of a dance move created in 2015 by viral star NL Vossi and the dance even features in the music video!

# TAKING GLASTONBURY BY STORM

In summer 2019, Stormzy became the first rapper to headline at Glastonbury Festival. As well as bringing the house down with his performance, he spoke out about the inequality he saw in society and in the arts. Stormzy brought his trademark charisma and energy to the set, but also invited other Black performers to the stage, including ballet dancers, a gospel choir and even a group of BMX riders! In an interlude, he listed over sixty grime artists that had either paved the way for him, or were active in the scene. Through this gesture, he shared his epic moment with many others.

However – though you'd never have known it if you were in the audience – all was not well on stage. Just twenty minutes into his performance, Stormzy's earpiece blew. Suddenly, he couldn't hear a thing – not the music, not the DJ and not even his own voice! Like a true professional, he carried on as if nothing was wrong, but inside he was panicking. He got through the set, but was convinced he'd messed up, big time. As he came off the stage, Stormzy broke down and couldn't stop crying for an hour!

He only calmed down when he saw some of the footage from the set and realized the faulty earpiece hadn't ruined anything. In fact, his performance was incredible. It would not only go down in Glastonbury's history, but British cultural history, too.

For his performance, Stormzy wore a customized stab vest, featuring a monochrome Union Jack. The vest was designed by anonymous street artist, Banksy, and was seen by many as a statement about the issue of knife crime in Britain.

In August 2019, Stormzy sadly broke up with his girlfriend, Maya Jama, after four years together. He moved to a new house in Kingston, West London, with his two pet Rottweilers for company.

# OWNING IT

Over the years, Stormzy had become good friends with pop sensation Ed Sheeran and towards the end of 2019, they released two singles together: "Take Me Back to London" and "Own It". The tracks did well in the charts ("Own It" hit number one!), but some people criticized Stormzy, saying he had sold out by collaborating with such a commercial artist. For Stormzy, however, it was about more than getting a hit. Though it might have seemed an unlikely match, he and Ed had good chemistry and a lot in common, from their musicality to their ambition. When they worked together, something just clicked.

# BECOMING A ROLE MODEL

In October, Stormzy appeared on *Time* magazine's front cover. Inside, he was listed as one of its "next generation leaders". He'd come a long way from his first YouTube videos with just a few hundred hits. The article recognized the massive influence Stormzy had on young people in Britain.

Though Stormzy is happy he can make a difference by using his voice, he sometimes struggles with the idea of being a role model. It worries him that a throwaway comment could make a headline the next day.

> **"Some days I don't want to be a role model, because some days I'm not a role model."**
>
> —Stormzy (*Rise Up*, 2018)

# HEAVY IS THE HEAD: A SECOND ALBUM

Unlike with *Gang Signs & Prayer*, Stormzy was unable to dedicate a solid block of time to his second album, *Heavy is the Head*. Instead, he squeezed in studio time while touring various locations across the globe, working with several different producers. Rather than telling his life story like in his first album, Stormzy wanted to speak about who he was now – the Stormzy in public and the Stormzy in private. He wanted to speak about the burden of being a superstar, being seen as a voice for young Black Britain, and all the responsibility that came with it.

The album was released on 13th December and quickly moved up the charts to number one, proving that the success of *Gang Signs & Prayer* had not been a fluke, but the start of an incredible career and musical journey.

## WHERE TO NEXT?

In February 2020, Stormzy took home another BRIT award for British Male Solo Artist.

In his acceptance speech, he gave thanks to God, his mum and his whole #Merky team.

He'd intended to spend much of 2020 on tour, but these plans were sadly put on hold due to the coronavirus (COVID-19) pandemic. Stormzy used the time in lockdown to hang out with his dogs and do more volunteer work, including partnering with The Good Guys (a decorating company) to redecorate the bedroom of a young fan as a special surprise!

From bursting on to the scene just a few years ago, Stormzy has come an incredibly long way in such a short space of time. Despite his confident lyrics and self-proclaimed title "king of grime", Stormzy remains humble.

He's thankful to those artists who came before him and broke down barriers so he could get where he is today. Whether it's another album, a sold-out tour, or an incredible viral video, whatever he goes on to next, the world will be waiting.

# INSPIRED BY ICONS

**Stage name:** Dizzee Rascal
**Real name:** Dylan Kwabena Mills
**Date of birth:** 18th September 1984

One of the great pioneers of grime music, Dizzee Rascal has achieved five number-one hits, including "Bonkers" and "Dance Wiv Me". He's won heaps of awards, including three MOBOs and a BRIT for British Male Solo Artist.

**Stage name:** Lethal Bizzle
**Real name:** Maxwell Owusu Ansah
**Date of birth:** 14th September 1984

Lethal Bizzle first appeared on the scene in 2002 as part of the grime group More Fire Crew, getting his first top ten with the single "Oi!". His debut solo single "Pow! (Forward)" was banned from the radio due to its violent lyrics, but still made number eleven on the UK singles charts.

stonbury, Stormzy namechecked the grime icons who had before him, making his journey possible, including **Giggs,** **e Rascal, Skepta, Ghetts, Kano, Wiley, Tinie Tempah** **thal Bizzle**, before moving on to an even longer list of grime stars he wanted the world to know about.

**Stage name:** Kano
**Real name:** Kane Brett Robinson
**Date of birth:** 21st May 1985

Kano has been a powerful presence in the grime scene since its early beginnings. His debut single "P's and Q's" was released way back in 2004 and was a big hit with underground grime fans. Known for his fast-paced rapping style and slick lyrics, he now has six studio albums under his belt. Beyond music, Kano took a starring role in Channel 4 drama *Top Boy*.

**Stage name:** Skepta
**Real name:** Joseph Junior Adenuga
**Date of birth:** 19th September 1982

Skepta became involved in the early grime scene, rapping, DJing and producing music. As the genre became more well known, Skepta established himself as one of the greatest grime artists of all time, creating hits including "That's Not Me" and "Shut Down".

Though grime was the genre he was most passionate about growing up, musicians of other genres have inspired Stormzy along the way, too. From incredible songwriters **Frank Ocean** and **Adele** to slick performers **Drake** and **Jay-Z**.

# STORMZY AND DAVE

Along with Stormzy, another artist whose impact goes beyond music is Dave. Still in his early twenties, he's already got a BRIT Award and a Mercury Prize for his debut album, **Psychodrama**. A classically trained pianist turned rapper, Dave is unafraid to put politics into his lyrics. Like Stormzy, he used his BRIT Awards performance to speak out about racism and the Conservative government. Performing his hit song, "Black", he spoke of his experiences as a young Black person in Britain.

Despite a number of people calling for him to "stick to music" he's not been put off from speaking about matters close to his heart. As artists like Dave and Stormzy continue to challenge and address the issues facing us today, they encourage their fans to do the same – to question the world around them and to stand up for what they believe in.

As well as being good friends, Dave joined Stormzy on stage at Glastonbury and Stormzy even made a cameo in Dave's music video for "Location". Surely, it's only a matter of time before they release a track together and make music gold.

**Stage name:** Dave (or Santan Dave)
**Real name:** David Orobosa Omoregie
**Date of birth:** 5th June 1998

A fan of nature documentaries, it's been announced that
Dave will join naturalist Sir David Attenborough for a special
episode of *BBC Earth*. Along with composer Hans Zimmer,
Dave will be playing piano on the soundtrack.

# FEATURING STORMZY

Over the years, Stormzy has collaborated with many incredible artists. From underground grime stars to household names, here are some of the musicians that have helped Stormzy take his work to even greater heights.

## KEHLANI

An admirer of her silky-smooth vocals, Stormzy invited the American singer-songwriter to join him on the track "Cigarettes & Cush".

# LILY ALLEN

Also featuring on "Cigarettes & Cush", Lily Allen provided her distinctive vocals for the chorus.

# ED SHEERAN

Ed and Stormzy became good friends early on in Stormzy's career. They first met at Ed's house in Sussex, where they spent the day playing music to each other. They've collaborated on two charting singles "Own It" and "Take Me Back to London" and have even treated fans to a few live performances together.

# LITTLE MIX

Stormzy provided a verse for the girl band's pop anthem "Power" and featured in the music video having his hair styled in an all-female barbershop.

## GHETTS

Stormzy joined forces with the older grime star on his track "Bad Boys".

# WRETCH 32

"Blinded by Your Grace Part 2" featured a collaboration with grime legend, Wretch 32, as well as a gospel choir.

# BURNA BOY

Nigerian singer and songwriter Burna Boy joined Stormzy on the catchy hit "Own It".

Though he's one of **Jay-Z**'s biggest fans, Stormzy actually turned down the opportunity of working with him on **"Take Me Back to London"**. He thought the American superstar wasn't a good fit for the track and worked up the nerve to say so while they were rehearsing. Luckily, Jay-Z understood and admired Stormzy's honesty! Stormzy still hopes that he'll get to work with his **"number one hero inspiration"** on a different track down the line though.

# FAMILY MATTERS

Stormzy didn't have it easy growing up. His family weren't well off, and his mum worked hard to provide for them all. Now Stormzy's a superstar, he's keen to repay her and his sisters for all they did for him. He's bought them designer clothes, phones and even cars!

In almost all of his acceptance speeches, Stormzy is quick to single out his mum for a heartfelt "thank you". Even though she may have wanted Stormzy to take the academic route and go to university, she's always been supportive of his dreams.

## RACHAEL ANSON

Like Stormzy, his big sister Rachael Anson is passionate about grime, and has become a successful DJ.

Stormzy and his mum appear in matching tracksuits in the video for "Know Me From". In the final cut, the pair walk confidently down the street together, but Stormzy said it took around thirty takes to get it right as his mum kept strutting into the shot too early or too late, or walking off in random directions. It looks like

# MAKING A DIFFERENCE

Stormzy is unafraid to call out injustice in society and wants to use his platform as a force for good. Here are just a few of the things he's doing to make a difference.

## SPEAKING OUT

In 2016, when the BRIT Awards failed to nominate any grime artists or, in fact, any British artists of colour, Stormzy called them out on it and even took a meeting with the event's chairman to address the issue.

## YOUR VOTE MATTERS

Before the 2019 General Election, Stormzy encouraged his followers to sign up to vote with a series of tweets. Voting registration spiked by 236 per cent that same day!

## STANDING UP FOR GRENFELL

After the Grenfell Tower fire, Stormzy provided a powerful opening verse for a charity single, expressing the pain and anger he felt at the disaster. The track, a cover of "Bridge Over Troubled Water", raised money for families of the victims of the fire.

## PROVIDING FUNDING

Stormzy continuously gives back to the community and supports other Black artists and creatives. In 2020, he made a pledge to donate £10 million over the next ten years in order tackle racial inequality and social injustices in the UK. Not long after, BBC Children in Need stepped in to match his pledge!

# THE STORMZY SCHOLARSHIP

In 2018, Stormzy launched a scholarship offering two financial grants to Black students admitted to the University of Cambridge. Students from minority backgrounds are still under-represented at the uni, and Stormzy wanted to do something to address that. He hoped that the scholarship would inspire his young fans who dreamed of going to a top university and help break down the barriers that might be stopping them from applying.

In June 2019, Stormzy's publishing imprint with Penguin Random House, #Merky Books, published *Taking Up Space: The Black Girl's Manifesto for Change* – written by Cambridge University graduates Chelsea Kwakye and Ore Ogunbiyi.

Examining the lack of diversity in higher education and the importance of including Black history in the academic curriculum – as well as their first-hand experiences and tips – they hoped their book would be a manifesto and guide for change.

Stormzy dreams of growing #Merky into something far bigger than music. With a publishing company, a record label and a scholarship programme already under the #Merky banner, it's exciting to think where Stormzy will take his brand next.

# REAL FANS

Despite his busy schedule, Stormzy always tries to make time for his fans. As well as holding book and album signings, visiting schools and chatting to his followers on social media, he goes above and beyond to let his dedicated fanbase know just how important they are to him.

## FREE CREPS

On the release of Wicked Skengman 4, Stormzy set out on to the streets of London with a car boot packed full of brand-new Adidas trainers to hand out to fans who had downloaded his new track.

## HELP ME OUT!

At each of his performances, Stormzy calls out to his screaming fans to help him out as he raps or sings his most popular tracks. The noise reverberating back as the audience join in is deafening!

# INSPIRING A GENERATION

In interviews, Stormzy often chats about his desire to inspire his fans to achieve their own dreams. In particular, he wants young Black men to know "you're better than anything anyone's ever told you that you are". He hopes that people will see his own rags-to-riches story as an example of what can be achieved through hard work and ambition.

# EPIC BIRTHDAY BASH

In 2016, Stormzy booked out the whole of Thorpe Park for his birthday! He held a competition on Twitter and invited 200 fans to join him and his friends for a day of fun.
As well as riding as many rollercoasters as they liked, the fans were treated to Adidas goodie bags, free Nandos and live performances – including one from Stormzy himself.

Two years later, Stormzy went one better, flying out a group of fans to a private villa in Menorca for his 25th birthday. He didn't actually tell the group where they were going until they got to the airport – only that they would need swimming costumes, sun cream and a phone charger!

At the villa, the day-long party soon got underway, with Stormzy's DJ sister Rachael Anson on the decks, inflatables in the pool, and unlimited food and drink! On the flight home, Stormzy kept everyone entertained by telling bad jokes over the PA.

# ALBUM ART

Like everything Stormzy has a hand in creating, the album covers for *Gang Signs & Prayer* and *Heavy is the Head* are striking and powerful.

On his first album cover, Stormzy stands at the centre of a long table, with people in balaclavas sitting either side in a pose that mirrors the famous painting *The Last Supper* by Leonardo da Vinci.

On his second album, Stormzy holds the customized stab vest from his Glastonbury performance, with the acronym for the album title, *h.i.t.h*, encircling his head like a crown of gold letters.

**Use this space to design your own eye-catching album art. You could create a cover for Stormzy's next release, or design what your own dream album would look like.**

# STREET STYLE

**From his signature tracksuits to his sophisticated suits, Stormzy always looks stylish. Here are some of his most iconic looks. Which is your favourite?**

Stormzy is regularly spotted sporting Adidas' stylish but comfortable tracksuits and trainers. He even had his own collaboration with the brand. In the video for "Shut Up" he dons a bold head-to-toe red tracksuit, but usually wears more muted tones like black, navy and grey.

Other than Adidas, Stormzy rarely wears obvious labels or brands, and instead sticks to plain, tight-fitting T-shirts or sweatshirts.

Though in general his style is casual, Stormzy doesn't mind dressing up in stylish suits for special occasions.

Stormzy's a style icon for many, but that doesn't mean he's beyond a fashion faux pas. He once appeared on BBC Breakfast wearing his slippers – he'd been in a rush to get out of the house and forgot to change into his trainers!

# STORMZY ON SCREEN

**Showing the world that his talent goes beyond music, Stormzy has also landed acting roles in two exciting shows.**

## BROTHERHOOD

Stormzy's first acting role came in 2016, when he featured in the final instalment of the *Hood* trilogy where he played Yardz.

## NOUGHTS AND CROSSES

In 2020, Stormzy appeared in an BBC adaptation of his favourite novel *Noughts and Crosses*, by Malorie Blackman. Stormzy played the role of Kolawale, an editor-in-chief at a national newspaper, a new role made just for him that didn't appear in the original book. He was a little nervous about the part at first, but soon found his stride and got great reviews.

Stormzy has always been very vocal about his respect and love for the *Noughts and Crosses* author – he raps about her in "Superheroes", saying *"I'm Malorie Blackman, the way I sell books"*. His publishing company, #Merky Books, will publish Malorie's autobiography in 2022.

# THE ULTIMATE QUIZ

Find out how well you know the king of grime with the ultimate Stormzy quiz. Circle your answers then turn to page 74 to discover your score!

**1.** What area of London did Stormzy grow up in?

| | |
|---|---|
| **A. North** | **B. East** |
| **C. South** | **D. West** |

**2.** What is Stormzy's mum's name?

| | |
|---|---|
| **A. Abigail** | **B. Anne** |
| **C. Amelia** | **D. Arya** |

**3.** What is Stormzy's favourite novel?

| | |
|---|---|
| **A. *The Hunger Games* by Suzanne Collins** | **B. *The Hate U Give* by Angie Thomas** |
| **C. *Northern Lights* by Philip Pullman** | **D. *Noughts and Crosses* by Malorie Blackman** |

**4.** What year did Stormzy release his *168* mixtape?

| | |
|---|---|
| **A. 2011** | **B. 2012** |
| **C. 2013** | **D. 2014** |

**5.** How many Wicked Skengman videos did Stormzy put up on YouTube?

| | |
|---|---|
| **A. 2** | **B. 4** |
| **C. 6** | **D. 8** |

**6.** Which two grime heavyweights does Stormzy give a shout out to in "Know Me From"?

| | |
|---|---|
| **A. Wiley and Dizzee Rascal** | **B. Skepta and Wiley** |
| **C. Dizzee Rascal and Lethal Bizzle** | **D. Lethal Bizzle and Skepta** |

**7.** How many copies did *Gang Signs & Prayer* sell in its first week?

| | |
|---|---|
| **A. Over 38,000** | **B. Over 48,000** |
| **C. Over 58,000** | **D. Over 68,000** |

**8.** In which song do these lyrics appear: *Mum, I save it all for you. Listen to the words I say. No more broken promises, I promise this, I'll save it all for you.*

A. "100 Bags"

B. "Know Me From"

C. "Cold"

D. "Big For Your Boots"

**9.** What was Stormzy's first number-one single?

A. "Dreamer's Disease"

B. "Blinded by Your Grace Part 2"

C. "Shut Up"

D. "Vossi Bop"

**10.** Which of these stars didn't join Stormzy on stage at his 2019 Glastonbury performance?

A. Chris Martin

B. Ed Sheeran

C. Fredo

D. Dave

**11.** Which university does Stormzy provide two scholarships for?

A. King's College London

B. Durham University

C. University of Oxford

D. University of Cambridge

**12.** Complete these lyrics from Stormzy's song "Crown": *I have my reasons and life has its lessons. I tried to be grateful and...*

| | |
|---|---|
| **A. go the right direction** | **B. pay attention** |
| **C. count my blessings** | **D. ask no questions** |

## Now flip the page to see the answers and add up your score!

Answers: 1. C; 2.A; 3.D; 4. C; 5. B; 6 A.; 7. D; 8. A; 9. D; 10. B; 11. D; 12. C

**0-4: Big for Your Boots**
It looks like you need to go back to basics! Brush up on your Stormzy knowledge then try again.

**5–7: Still Disappointed**
Not bad, but not great either. You know some stuff about the king of grime but there's definitely room for improvement.

**8–12: Wicked Skengman**
You're a true fan! From rapping along to every track to stalking his social media, you're up to date on all things Stormzy.

# FOLLOW STORMZY'S FOOTSTEPS

Dreaming of a life in the spotlight like Stormzy?
As well as talent, you'll need perseverance,
dedication and a bit of luck, too.

## LOVE WHAT YOU DO

Rather than wanting to become famous for the sake of it, you should be passionate about what you do. If you love making music, then make it regardless of whether it might one day get you money or glory. As Stormzy says, "you shouldn't want to be a celebrity, but do something you love".

## LIFT OTHERS UP

Getting to the top doesn't mean you have to knock other people down along the way. In the past, Stormzy's hired his schoolfriends as members of his team to help them achieve their own dreams. He also supports other contemporary artists, as well as older musicians that paved the way for him. See if you can get your friends involved in your plans or collaborate with other people that share your passion.

# PUT IN THE HOURS

Stormzy didn't get a number one overnight. It took years of writing, practising, filming videos and doing promotions before he started getting airtime on the radio. There's no quick way to achieve your dreams – the more time you put into creating, the more you'll get out of it.

# BE BOLD

Even if you're nervous, put yourself out there. Whether it's performing to a small group of friends, taking part in a rap battle or filming a video for social media, you've got to start somewhere. Ask your audience what they thought, and take on board their advice for improving, even if it's hard to hear.

# STAY TRUE TO YOURSELF

While it's important to listen to feedback, it's also important to trust your instincts and follow your heart. Don't let yourself be pigeon-holed by other people. If you want to try a new music style or a new look, go for it, no matter what other people say you should or shouldn't do.

# WRITE YOUR OWN BARS

Stormzy's powerful lyrics often balance humour with hard-hitting political points, emotional reflections with confident statements.

# BE INSPIRED

With Stormzy's lines as inspiration, use these next pages to have a go at writing your own lyrics.

# INDEX

# PICTURE CREDITS

While every effort has been made to credit all contributors, we would like to apologize should there be any omissions or errors, and would be pleased to make any appropriate corrections for future editions of this book.

Internal images (from left to right on page):
P4 ADRIAN DENNIS/Gettyimages, Gareth Cattermole/Gettyimages, Gareth Cattermole/Gettyimages, Gareth Cattermole/Gettyimages; P7 Karwai Tang/Gettyimages, Jim Dyson/Gettyimages; P8 Samir Hussein/Gettyimages; P11 Frank Hoensch/Gettyimages; P12 Gareth Cattermole/Gettyimages; P13 Frank Hoensch/Gettyimages; P14 Paul Bergen/Gettyimages; P17 Samir Hussein/Gettyimages; P18 Gareth Cattermole/Gettyimages; P19 Samir Hussein/Gettyimages; P20 Gareth Cattermole/Gettyimages; P22 ADRIAN DENNIS/Gettyimages; P23 Gareth Cattermole/Gettyimages; P24 Samir Hussein/Gettyimages; P26 David Wolff – Patrick/Gettyimages, Frank Hoensch/Gettyimages; P27 Joseph Okpako/Gettyimages; P29 John Phillips/Gettyimages; P31 Jim Dyson/Gettyimages; P33 Paul Bergen/Gettyimages; P34 PYMCA/Gettyimages; P36 Frank Hoensch/Gettyimages; P37 David Wolff – Patrick/Gettyimages; P38 Samir Hussein/Gettyimages; P40 Rune Hellestad – Corbis/Gettyimages; P41 Visionhaus/Gettyimages; P42 Ollie Millington/Gettyimages; P43 Taylor Hill/Gettyimages; P44 David M. Benett/Gettyimages; P45 Dave J Hogan/Gettyimages; P46 Scott Legato/Gettyimages; P47 Roger Kisby/Gettyimages, Mike Marsland/Gettyimages; P48 Steve Rogers Photography/Gettyimages, Kevin Mazur/Gettyimages; P49 Amy Sussman/Gettyimages, Joseph Okpako/Gettyimages; P50 Tabatha Fireman/Gettyimages; P51 Gareth Cattermole/Gettyimages; P52 Jim Dyson/Gettyimages; P55 PYMCA/Gettyimages; P56 OLI SCARFF/Gettyimages; p57 Samir Hussein/Gettyimages; P58 PYMCA/Gettyimages, Gareth Cattermole/Gettyimages, Ross Gilmore/Gettyimages; P61 Frank Hoensch/Gettyimages; P62 Shirlaine Forrest/Gettyimages, Shirlaine Forrest/Gettyimages; P64 Shirlaine Forrest/Gettyimages; P65 David M. Benett/Gettyimages, David M. Benett/Gettyimages, David M. Benett/Gettyimages; P67 Mike Marsland/Gettyimages, Karwai Tang/Gettyimages; P71 Karwai Tang/Gettyimages; P74 Gareth Cattermole/Gettyimages; P75 Joseph Okpako/Gettyimages; P76 Samir Hussein/Gettyimages; p77 PYMCA/Gettyimages